Robert R. Carkhuff, Ph.D.
CARKHUFF INSTITUTE OF HUMAN TECHNOLOGY

Copyright © 1974, 1985 by
Human Resource Development Press, Inc.

22 Amherst Rd.
Amherst, Masasachusetts 01002 (413) 253-3488
1-800-822-2801

Bernice R. Carkhuff, Publisher
Elizabeth Grose, Editor

Library of Congress Cataloging in Publication Data
International Standard Book Number 0-87425-020-X

Cover Design by Dorothy Fall
Word processing by Susan Kotzin
Composition by Magazine Group
Printing and Binding by Bookcrafters

ABOUT THE AUTHOR

Dr. Robert R. Carkhuff is the most-referenced counseling psychologist according to Division 17, American Psychological Association. He is Chairman, Carkhuff Institute of Human Technology, a non-profit institute dedicated to the development and implementation of human resource development, training and performance programs in home, school, work and community settings.

The American Institute for Scientific Information ranks Dr. Carkhuff as the second youngest of the 100 most-cited social scientists, including such historical figures as Dewey, Freud and Marx. He is also author of three of the 100 most-referenced texts, including his two-volume classic, *Helping and Human Relations*.

Dr. Carkhuff is known as the originator of helping models and human resource development skills programs. He is also parent of the Human Technology movement which emphasizes models, systems and technologies for individual performance and organizational productivity. His most recent books on the topics of human resource development and productivity are *Sources of Human Productivity* and *The Exemplar: the Exemplary Performer in the Age of Productivity*.

PREFACE

Program development lets us minimize and ultimately, rise above our human limitations. It enables us to achieve goals we once only imagined reaching. And just as program development has made it possible for human beings to walk in space, it allows us to walk proudly on earth: strong, healthy, skilled and productive.

Productive Program Development is based upon *The Art of Program Development*, first published over a decade ago and used by tens of thousands of readers to develop living, learning and working programs.

For those of us who care about helping ourselves and others, for parents and children, teachers and students, counselors and clients, employers and employees, program development makes all things possible. It is where all of us begin; where we end up depends only upon the program we develop.

Any goal that can be operationalized can be achieved. Our goals in space or on earth are limited only by the boundaries of our intellect.

Washington, D.C.   R.R.C.
May, 1985

Putting a Person on the Moon: An Image of Program Development

NASA had the goal of putting a person on the moon. Its staff spent years exploring the available data and attempting to understand the goal. Finally, Dr. John Houbolt defined the objective in operational terms. He separated the lunar-landing mission into precise components, functions and processes. The programs and systems were designed, improved and implemented to achieve the objective. Thus, the spacecraft orbited the moon by the same processes that it orbited the Earth. Then the astronauts entered the lunar module and separated from the command module to make the lunar descent. Finally, the lunar module fired its rocket engine to make the lunar landing. In so doing, NASA operationalized putting a person on the moon—a triumph that was a product of humankind's most vivid imagination.

The story of the lunar landing illustrates the principles of productive program development: exploring, understanding and acting upon programs; defining objectives; developing programs; sequencing the program; designing program systems; implementing programs. Program development recycles operational steps in a continuous attempt to improve our ability to achieve our objectives.

If we can put a person on the moon with our program development skills, can we do less here on Earth? Can we do less for children and parents in a constantly changing world or for learners and teachers with a constantly changing curriculum? Can we do less for employees and employers in an Information Society? Every person is exceptional and can be an exceptional performer with program development skills. Any goal that can be conceived can be defined. And any goal that can be defined can be achieved with program development skills.

PPD
PRODUCTIVE PROGRAM DEVELOPMENT
DEVELOPMENT
Table of Contents

1

PPD

INTRODUCTION

Programs are universal. All of nature is programmed. Our very human natures are programmed, although we do not always understand the programs. Sometimes when we do understand them, we do not like them. For us as humans, there are good programs and bad programs. We can even say that there are programs where the schedules of steps appear random. The issue for us, as humans, is intervention. Do we wish to intervene in the ongoing programs? Do we wish to extend the quantity and quality of our lives? Do we intend to generate our own programs?

Productive Program Development

Productive program development involves caring. It means we care enough to attempt to insure success in achieving our human goals. Programs are simply the price we pay for the things we care about. Programs mean we do not want to fail. Things matter to us. We want to win.

The effects of programs are cumulative. When we intervene programmatically to achieve a goal, we not only increase the desire to achieve another goal. We also increase the probability of achieving another goal. Similarly, when we are non-programmatic, we decrease the success, the desire and the probability of achieving another goal. Clearly, the quantity and quality of our programs dictate the quantity and quality of our lives.

There are an infinite number of ways to lose, and they are all non-programmatic and non-productive. Some people live brief lives making a specialty of defining new ways of losing. We see this everyday in new fads in all areas of human endeavor—not only in various fields of creativity and irrational lifestyles but also in personal relationships, and within groups, societies and nations. The implications are profound. People who subtract, detract, or distract ultimately destroy themselves and others, whether slowly or quickly.

Programs Have Implications

There is only one way to win, achieve, or be successful in accomplishing one's objectives, and that is programmatically. Productive people design and implement programs which will most accurately satisfy their own values, and the requirements of the environment in which they function. Productive people develop productive programs which achieve their goals most effectively and most efficiently.

PPD Skills

Productive program development skills emphasize the following: defining the objective; developing the programmatic tasks, steps, check steps, and criteria needed to achieve the objective; and implementing the program. The definition of the objective and the development and implementation of the program enable us to achieve important goals in our lives. Together, these activities define PPD skills.

Productive program development skills begin with processing information. They are the critical ingredient of the action phase of processing. People explore where they are in relation to their experience. People understand where they want or need to be. People act to get from where they are to where they want or need to be. PPD skills provide the programs for people in the action phase of processing.

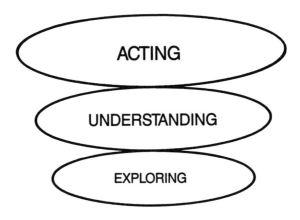

Acting Upon Programs

The objective is defined by the operations needed to achieve it. These operations define the following: *who* the operators are; *what* operations they are performing; *how* and *why* they are performing these operations; *where* and *when* they are performing these operations; *how well* they are performing these operations. This operational definition of the objective defines the programs that are developed and implemented to achieve the objective.

Defining the Objective

The programs are derived from the operational definition of the objective. More precisely, they are derived from the processes by which the operations are implemented, i.e., *how* the operations are performed. The programs are comprised of the tasks needed to achieve the objectives. In turn, the tasks are comprised of the steps necessary to perform the tasks. Check steps aid us in performing the tasks correctly and completely. Criteria of milestones and timelines aid in defining guidelines for performing the tasks. Finally, mastery of the tasks facilitates implementation of the program. Together, these program tasks define program development.

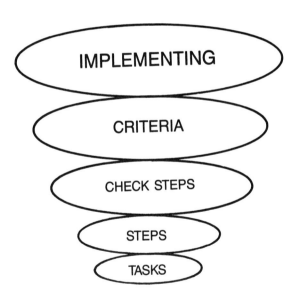

PPD, then, is the programmatic means we employ to achieve operational definitions. The means and the ends are integrally related. The operational definition describes the processes from which the programs are derived. The programs define the achievement of the objective. Productive program development is the development of the most effective and efficient means for achieving the objective.

2
PREPARING
FOR ACTING

Freeze! That's right—Freeze! Don't move a muscle! Freeze your body! Now take a look at yourself.

Just a moment ago, you turned the page of this book. You thought you were reading. But were you really? Let's take a look. Look at yourself as others see you. Look at your "frozen" body.

Note your posture! Are you erect? Slouched? Slumped? Leaning forward? Sideways? Crooked? How much? How far? Get a good index of where you are. Because that is where every program begins. You cannot know where you are going if you do not know the point at which you start.

Programs Begin With Exploring

If you know where you are, then you can determine where you want or need to be. Were you satisfied with your reading posture? Do you want to learn how to posture yourself most effectively for giving your full and undivided attention to reading? If so, then you will set a goal to develop an attentive reading posture. A goal is defined by the behaviors you have to perform to achieve it. We may define the goal of developing an attentive reading posture as sitting or standing erectly, being squared-off with the material, and leaning toward the material at a 10° to 20° angle. You are now ready to develop a simple program for attentive reading posture.

Programs are Mediated by Understanding

If you know where you are and where you want or need to be, it remains only for you to develop a program to get there. Programs are the steps you take to get to your goal. One way of outlining the steps of a program is to simply arrange the behaviors of your goal from most simple to most complex. For example, you may arrange your attentive reading posture program as follows: most simple behavior, squaring off with the material; most complex behavior, leaning toward the material; intermediary behavior, sitting erectly. You now have the outline of a simple program to develop an attentive reading posture.

Programs Conclude With Acting

Obviously, attentive posture is not all you need to read effectively. But it is an early goal in an effective reading program. It will also serve to introduce you to what I expect of you when you read this book. My goal is to help you learn the skills of program development. To get yourself ready to learn, you must first pay attention to the material. Therefore, I expect you to assume an attentive reading posture as your first step in this learning program. As you read this book, I also expect you to keep in mind the simple steps of program development that you went through to develop your attentive reading posture program.

These steps introduce you to the basic ingredients of program development. You may review them now: 1) Defining the objective; 2) Developing program steps; 3) Sequencing program steps; 4) Designing program systems; 5) Implementing program steps. Learning to develop these program development skills is the goal of our program. You will have to involve yourself in a developmental learning process in order to achieve this goal.

The Learning Goal

In order to learn to develop program development skills, you must first explore where you are. You must explore where you are from your own internal frame of reference. This way you know how you see yourself in relation to your world. You must also explore where you are from an outside or external frame of reference. That way you know how the world sees you. These assessments must be observable and measurable. And in the event that there is a discrepancy between where you see yourself and where you are seen, you will learn to close that gap.

Exploring Where You Are

When you have explored where you are, then you are ready to attempt to understand where you are in relation to where you want to be. The motivation for achieving your goal comes from your personal frame of reference. You define your goal in terms of where you want to be. Then you break it down further in terms of where you need to be in order to get to where you want to be. To define where you need to be, you break your goals down into their observable and measurable operations so that you can achieve them.

Understanding Where You Want to Be

When you understand where you are in relation to where you want and need to be, then you are ready to attempt to get there. You develop a step-by-step program to get from where you are to where you want and need to be. You develop each step of the program carefully in order to outline the way to get to your goal. You draw your observable and measurable steps from your definition of your goal. This is because you have defined your goal in terms of the operations necessary to achieve it. You line these steps up in some systematic way to lead to your goal. Now you have a program for achieving your goal. Observable and measurable steps to a goal, sequenced systematically, are called programs. You will go on to develop sub-steps to achieve each of your steps. In that way you insure the success of your program in achieving your goal.

Acting to Get There

Programs, then, are simply the steps you take to get from where you are to where you want to be. They begin with your personal frame of reference and move toward achievable goals. For instance, while reading this book, everything you do influences how well you will achieve your goals, even your attentive reading posture! Every behavior counts. In other words, if you miss a step, you could fall into a hole. Deviate from the step and you lose sight of your goal. You are either doing all the little things that count, or you are doing nothing at all! You are either succeeding or you are failing.

Productive Program Development

Exploring Experience

All effective programs begin with exploring where you are. In other words, effective programs begin with the input of the people who are to be affected by the program. If the programs begin with your frame of reference, then they take you into consideration. And, in turn, you are motivated to make them succeed. If the programs do not begin with your frame of reference, then they do not take you into consideration. And your resulting lack of motivation dooms them to failure. There are two critical dimensions of exploring human experience: 1) exploring where you think you are; 2) exploring where you really are. These are the learning objectives of exploring where you are.

For example, Ray tended to overrate his physical, emotional and intellectual functioning. When he tested himself out, he was surprised to find that he functioned below survival level physically in terms of his cardiorespiratory coordination, endurance, strength and flexibility. In turn, although he had thought of himself as a productive initiator emotionally and interpersonally, he found that he did not always attend to people or other sources of information. Finally, he found that he was functioning more at the conceptual than at the skills level intellectually: he had the words but not the behavior. Ray needed to explore himself more in order to get an accurate picture of where he was.

"I feel dissatisfied with my performance."

Exploring Where You Think You Are

On the other hand, June was quite accurate in her own self-assessments. She found that the objective assessments validated her own picture of herself. She was functioning at a level of adaptability physically: she had enough energy to make it through each day. Interpersonally, she could respond accurately to other people's expressions. Intellectually, she could define objectives although she was deficit in the program development skills to achieve the objectives. June had a good picture of where she was as a starting point in program development.

Understanding Goals

The only reason for a program is to achieve a goal. A goal tells you where you want to be. In some way, it is worthwhile for you, and you are motivated to achieve it. But, it is not enough to understand where you want to be. You must also understand where you need to be in order to get to where you want to be. This means that you must define your goal in terms of the specific steps you need to take to get to your goal. These are the learning objectives of understanding human goals: 1) understanding where you want to be; 2) understanding where you need to be.

For example, Ray was determined to improve his over-all level of functioning, physically, emotionally and intellectually. He selected the goal area in which he was functioning at relatively the highest level. That gave him the highest probability of succeeding. He decided to attempt to improve his overall physical endurance. Ray had a good picture of where he needed to be.

"I feel disappointed because I can't function here and I really want to learn to do so."

Understanding Where You Need to Be

In turn, June was committed to improving her overall level of functioning. She decided to become even stronger in the emotional and interpersonal areas. That way she could contribute more to the people around her. June had a good picture of where she wanted to be.

"I feel excited about where I am and eager to improve."

Understanding Where You Want to Be

Acting Upon Programs

Now, finally, you are ready to develop your program. Developing a program simply means developing the steps to achieve a goal. A program is any means used to reach a goal. The best program is one where each step moves systematically toward the goal. Systematic programs allow you to know at each step how much you have mastered and how close you are to the goal. Systematic programs are created by developing the steps and sub-steps which are needed to achieve the goal. Developing the 1) primary, secondary and intermediary tasks and steps and 2) the check sub-steps and criteria for performance are the learning objectives for acting upon human programs.

For example, Ray was able to develop a program for running to build up his endurance. His initial goal was running a mile in ten minutes. His primary tasks for achieving the goal were as follows: walking, walking a mile, running a mile. Ray would later learn to develop the other tasks and steps he needed to achieve his goal.

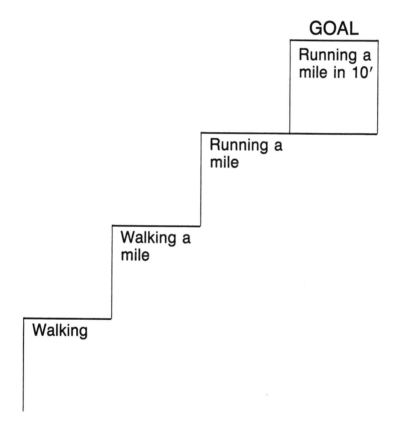

GOAL

Running a mile in 10′

Running a mile

Walking a mile

Walking

Acting to Get to Where You Need to Be

In a similar manner, June was able to develop her program for learning to personalize the understanding of problems or goals of other people. That way, she could contribute more to their welfare. Her initial goal was learning to understand the goals of others. Her primary tasks for achieving the goal were as follows: personalizing meaning, personalizing problems, personalizing goals. June would later learn to develop the other steps she needed to achieve her goal.

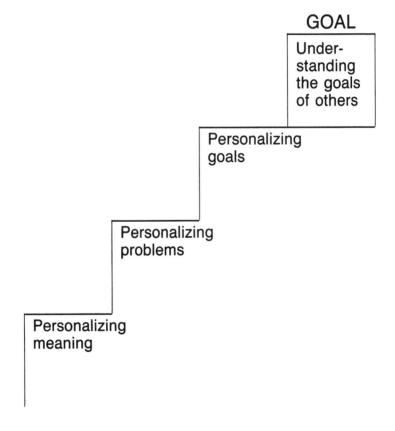

GOAL

Under-
standing
the goals
of others

Personalizing
goals

Personalizing
problems

Personalizing
meaning

Acting to Achieve Your Goal

You may wish to attempt to apply these processing skills to developing your own or someone else's program. You may pair up or work in triads with one person as helper, one as helpee and one as "trainer." Simply attempt to explore where you are in any area of physical functioning. You may use Table 1 on the following page to check your accuracy. Next, attempt to develop an understanding of a direction or goal that you would like to achieve in the area. Finally, develop the primary tasks needed to achieve the goal. You may, if you wish, design an exercise program to increase your endurance and cardio-respiratory coordination. Seek help from other sources of expertise, if necessary.

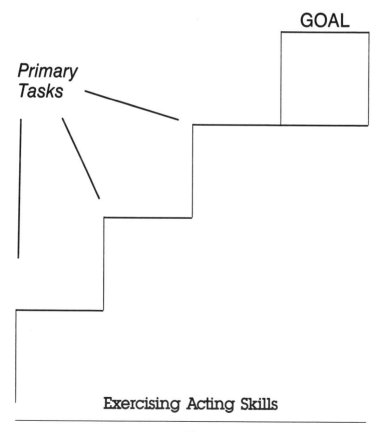

GOAL

Primary Tasks

Exercising Acting Skills

TABLE 1
PHYSICAL FUNCTIONING

LEVELS OF FUNCTIONING	CARDIO-RESPIRATORY (Pulse rate for 2 min) (after exercise)		ENDURANCE (Miles in 12 min)		STRENGTH (Situps in 2 min)		FLEXIBILITY (Toe Touch)
	Male	Female	Male	Female	Male	Female	Male and Female
5.0 Stamina	71	86	2.3	2.1	100	50	Palms on floor
4.5	89	95	2.0	1.9	97	35	Fists on floor
4.0 Intensity	115	120	1.8	1.7	61	27	2nd joint on floor
3.5	132	137	1.6	1.5	52	24	Fingertips on floor
3.0 Adaptability	158	163	1.5	1.4	47	20	Fingertips on toes
2.5	184	189	1.4	1.3	39	16	Fingertips to ankles
2.0 Intensity	201	206	1.2	1.1	34	14	Fingertips 10" below knees
1.5	227	232	1.1	1.0	26	9	Fingertips to knees
1.0 Intensity	245	250	1.0	.9	0	0	Fingertips above knees

In summary, initially, we attempt to explore ourselves in order to know where we are in relation to our experience. Then, we attempt to understand our goals in order to know where we are going. Finally, we attempt to develop programs in order to get from where we are to where we want or need to be. We develop the programs by determining the goal and developing the tasks and steps needed to achieve the goal. Productive program development skills can prepare us for achieving any goals.

3
DEFINING
OBJECTIVES

Not all objectives begin with a clearly organized diagnosis and definition. Many objectives begin with complex problem analyses and goal syntheses. Sometimes the direction to the goal is clear. Other times, the person must engage in problem-solving. The objective may then become the goal of the preferred course of action. In either event, an objective is characterized by the operations that comprise it. The dimensions of these operations include components, functions, processes, conditions and standards. These are observable and measurable dimensions. When fully implemented, they define the achievement of the objective.

Defining Objectives

For example, Ann's problem of overextending herself may be analyzed in operational terms:

Ann in relation to others assumes responsibilities by overextending herself, so that she can satisfy everyone at home, school and work, to the point where she fails to fully discharge any responsibilities.

Ann's self-defeating behavior is analyzed in fully operational terms. The terms cover the basic interrogatives of operations. They are observable and measurable.

Who? — Ann in relation to others

What? — assumes responsibilities

How? — by over extending herself

Why? — so that she can satisfy everyone

Where & When? — at home, school and during work hours

How well? — to the point where she fails to fully discharge any responsibilities

In the same manner, the new goals for Ann may be synthesized in operational terms:

Ann in relation to others will assume responsibilities by making-cost beneficial decisions, so that she can be productive at home, school and work, at the level where she can discharge all of her responsibilities at highly productive levels.

Again, Ann's goals are synthesized in the operational terms of the basic interrogatives:

Who?	— Ann in relation to others
What?	— will asssume responsibilities
How?	— by making cost-beneficial decisions
Why?	— so that she can be productive
Where & When?	— at home, school and during work hours
How well?	— at the level where she can discharge all of her responsibilities at highly productive levels

Defining Goals

Components

Components are the parts or participants of a phenomenon. They are usually labeled by nouns or the
names that we attach to people or things. Sometimes
we refer to components as the parts that comprise the
finished product when assembled or the complete ser-
vice when configured. Invariably, in developing human
objectives, the components are people who participate
in the phenomenon—initiators and recipients alike. For
example, Ann and the people to whom she relates are
the components of her performance improvement
program.

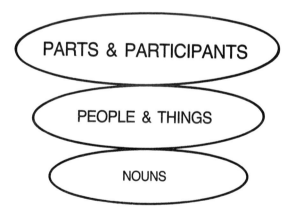

Defining Components

Similarly, June is the responder and other people are the recipients in her personalizing objective.

Ray's situation, however, is another story. While he is indeed the critical component in his endurance objective, there are other "thing" components that are critical in its definition, e.g. the running track or place, running gear and a stop watch. In a very real sense, these things are "participants" in Ray's running program. Whenever materials, machinery equipment or other critical "thing" resources are involved, they are integral to the definition of the components. For example, a computer or other processing machinery requires definition as a component along with the user. Thus, components define both *who* and *what* is involved in a given phenomenon.

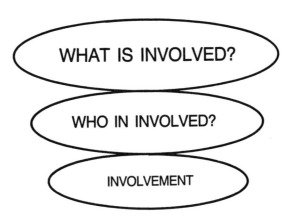

WHAT IS INVOLVED?

WHO IN INVOLVED?

INVOLVEMENT

Defining Involvement

Functions

Functions are the activities or purposes of a phenomenon. They are usually verbs that describe the actions or behaviors of the components. For example, we may say that people *think*, computers *process* and machines *assemble*. Ann's function was to learn to assume responsibilities.

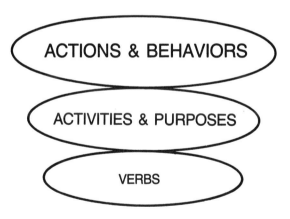

Defining Functions

Similarly, Ray's function is to develop his endurance. June's function is to learn to understand the experiences of others. Other "people" functions might include anything that people *do*, *know* or *feel* i.e., the skills, knowledge and attitudes needed to perform a response. In conjunction with people, other "thing" functions might include producing products, providing services or delivering benefits.

Defining Actions

Processes

Processes are the methods or procedures by which the functions are accomplished. They are usually adverbs that modify the functional activities or purposes. In other words, processes describe the means by which the functions are achieved. For example, we may say that people think by using their mind to process, computers process by digital techniques, and machines assemble by mechanical means. Ann's processes emphasized learning to make cost-beneficial decisions. Along with describing the methods and procedures, the processes also describe the reasons or personal meaning of performing the functions. Thus, people can learn to think in such a way as to become more effective and efficient in processing. Similarly, Ann learns to make cost-beneficial decisions in order to live her life more productively.

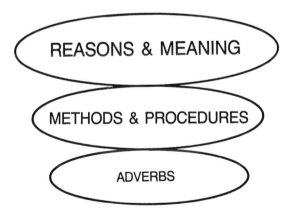

Defining Processes

In the same manner, Ray is developing his endurance by the process of walking and running. Similarly, June is learning to understand the experiences of others through the process of responding and personalizing. Both have reasons for accomplishing their functions. Ray wants to develop his endurance in order to improve his cardio-respiratory coordination. June wants to develop her understanding so that she can relate more productively to others.

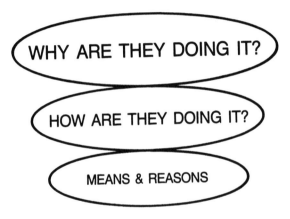

Defining Means and Reasons

Conditions

Conditions are the contexts or environments within which the functions take place. The conditions have two primary dimensions: place and time. Thus, conditions are adverbs which define *where* and *when* the functions take place, i.e., the parameters within which the functions may be achieved or discharged. For example, the people may think at home, the computers may process in school, and the machines may assemble at work. Ann's conditions involved making cost-beneficial decisions at home, school and work.

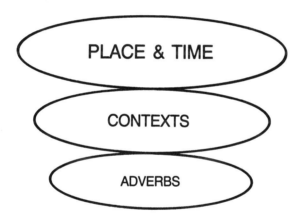

PLACE & TIME

CONTEXTS

ADVERBS

Defining Conditions

Likewise, Ray is developing his cardio-respiratory endurance by running at the community track after working hours. June is developing her understanding of others in all of the areas of her life—home, school and work. Both are establishing the parameters within which their functions may be achieved.

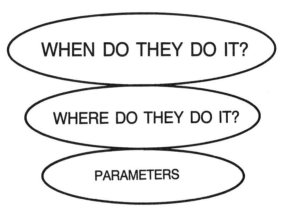

Standards

Standards are the criteria or indices by which the functions may be judged. They are adverbs that describe the levels of performance or excellence to be achieved by the functions. Thus, they describe *how well* the functions must be performed. For example, the people, computers and machines may all learn to process at high levels of productivity, i.e., minimizing resource investments and maximizing results outputs. Ann's standards emphasized discharging all of her responsibilities at highly productive levels.

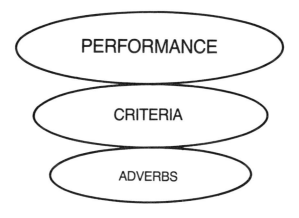

PERFORMANCE

CRITERIA

ADVERBS

Defining Standards

Thus, Ray's standards for improving his cardio-respiratory functioning may involve running the mile in ten minutes and/or reducing his pulse rate to under 160 for two minutes after exercise. June, in turn, may set standards for understanding others that involve being able to personalize meaning, problems and goals after making six interchangeable responses to human experience. Both are establishing the levels of excellence in performance to which they aspire.

Defining Excellence

We may now summarize Ray's definition of his objective:

Components	— Ray
Functions	— will develop his endurance
Processes	— by walking and running so that he will improve his cardio-respiratory coordination
Conditions	— at the community track after
Standards	— working hours at levels reducing his pulse rate to under 160 for two minutes after exercise

Ray's objective is now defined in terms of observable and measurable dimensions. The objective is now achievable.

In the same manner, we may summarize June's definition of her objective:

Components	—	June in relation to others
Functions	—	will learn to understand others
Processes	—	by personalizing so that she can relate more productively
Conditions	—	at home, school and work
Standards	—	at levels that personalize the goals of others

June's objective is now defined in terms that make it achievable through program development.

You may wish to define one of your own objectives in operational terms. You may continue to work with one of the physical dimensions which you have already processed or you may choose from one of the physical, emotional or intellectual areas in Table 2 on the following page. Explore, understand and prepare to act to rehabilitate a problem or improve your functioning in the area. Rate your level of functioning in the relevant area. You may seek a goal at the level above your current functioning. Seek expertise if you require further explication of the areas or levels. Then define your objective in operational terms.

Components

Functions

Processes

Conditions

Standards

Exercising Defining Skills

TABLE 2
LEVELS OF OVERALL FUNCTIONING

AREAS OF FUNCTIONING

LEVELS OF FUNCTIONING	PHYSICAL (Cardio-vascular, endurance, strength, flexibility)	EMOTIONAL (Interpersonal Processing)	INTELLECTUAL (Intellectual Processsing)
5–LEADER	STAMINA Functioning with intensity and stamina	INITIATING Able to initiate to help others to resolve problems and achieve goals	PROGRAMS Able to develop programs to achieve objectives
4–CONTRIBUTOR	INTENSITY Functioning with selective intensity	PERSONALIZING Able to personalize problems and goals of others	OBJECTIVES Able to define objectives in operational terms
3–PARTICIPANT	ADAPTABILITY Functioning adequately without intensity	RESPONDING Accurately responsive to others' experience	PRINCIPLES Able to account for relations between people and/or things
2–OBSERVER	SURVIVAL Barely able to make it through the day	ATTENDING Attentive to others	CONCEPT Able to identify relations between people and/or things
1–DETRACTOR	SICKNESS Unable to make it through the day	NONATTENDING Inattentive to others	FACTS Able to identify the labels we attach to people and things

In summary, we define our objectives in terms of the operations that comprise them.

Components — *Who* and *what* is involved?

Functions — *What* do they do?

Processes — *How* and *why* do they do it?

Conditions — *Where* and *when* do they do it?

Standards — *How well* do they do it?

These dimensions are observable, measurable and, therefore, achievable through program development. Productive defining scales prepare us for productive program development skills.

Productive Defining Skills

4

DEVELOPING TASKS

Let us set a simple objective. Suppose for the moment we are in our rooms and we would like to go to town or the college center or the library. Take a little time to design the major tasks you must perform, or the things you must do, in order to reach your destination.

Developing Tasks

You may be surprised how easy this assignment seems. But you may also be surprised at your failure to complete it satisfactorily. Below is a typical program of tasks for reaching the destination. Compare your program with it.

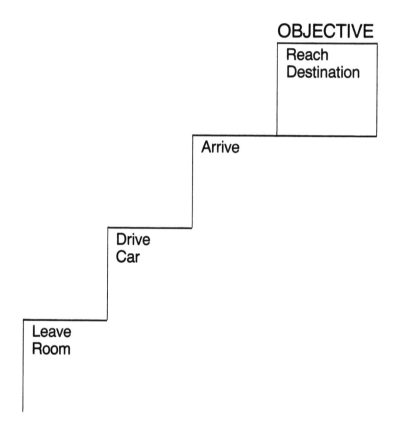

OBJECTIVE

Reach Destination

Arrive

Drive Car

Leave Room

Typical Tasks

Here is a sample of critical tasks which I must perform in order to achieve my objective of reaching the library and accessing materials. Each task involves the performance of a series of responses emphasizing critical skills, knowledge and attitudes.

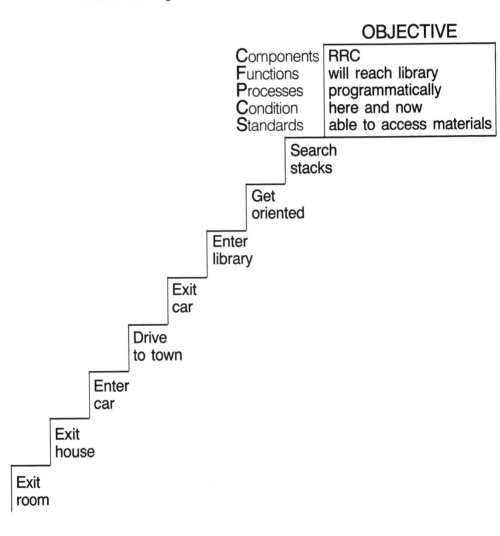

OBJECTIVE

Components	RRC
Functions	will reach library
Processes	programmatically
Condition	here and now
Standards	able to access materials

Search
stacks

Get
oriented

Enter
library

Exit
car

Drive
to town

Enter
car

Exit
house

Exit
room

Productive Tasks

In this context, each task can be defined in further detail just as we defined the objectives. For example, I may define the objective of exiting my room in terms of the operational dimensions that comprise this task:

Components — RRC

Functions — will exit the room

Processes — by reaching and opening the door so that he can leave

Conditions — here and now

Standards — at a level where he is able to open door ahead of him

Program development is the art and science of getting from one place to another. We may be moving physically. However, we may also move emotionally or intellectually. Program development is a science because we must describe, predict and control ourselves and our environments. It is an art because our programs begin and end with human experience. All programs begin with tasks.

Beginning With Tasks

Tasks

Tasks are the things we must perform in order to achieve our objectives. They are the real life applications of the skills, knowledge and attitudes we have acquired. Tasks include primary, secondary and intermediary tasks. The primary are the critical tasks we must perform. The secondary are the tasks that enable the performance of the primary tasks. Intermediary tasks are the tasks that bridge the gaps between primary and/or secondary tasks.

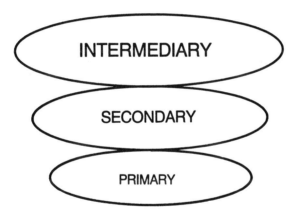

Primary Tasks

Primary tasks, then, are the critical tasks to be performed. They should always involve the first and last tasks. Often, they involve other tasks. The first task is usually the simplest, and the last task is usually the most complex. The other primary tasks are those which are critical to the performance of the most complex task.

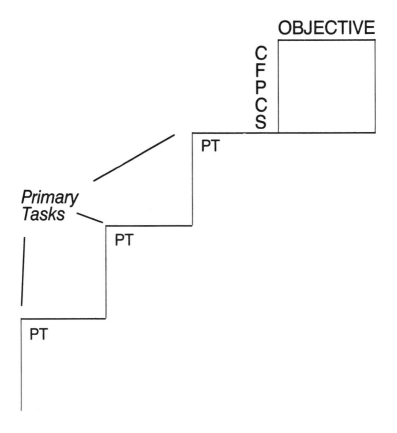

Developing Primary Tasks

For example, recall that Ray's primary tasks involved walking, walking a mile and running a mile. The last task was the most complex task leading to his goal of running a mile in 10 minutes. Also recall that June's primary tasks emphasized personalizing meaning, problems and goals. Ann's primary tasks for making cost-beneficial decisions are illustrated below:

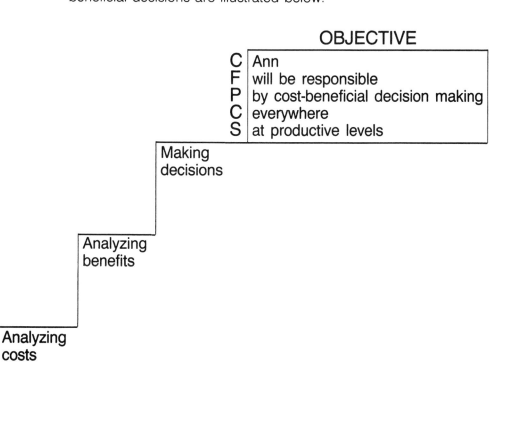

OBJECTIVE

C	Ann
F	will be responsible
P	by cost-beneficial decision making
C	everywhere
S	at productive levels

Making decisions

Analyzing benefits

Analyzing costs

Illustrating Primary Tasks

Secondary Tasks

Secondary tasks are enabling tasks. They enable the primary tasks to be performed. As a consequence, they generally precede the critical primary tasks. They are sequenced so that each task is contingent upon the completion of a previous task. We can most productively develop secondary tasks by treating the primary tasks as if they were objectives and developing the secondary tasks needed to achieve these objectives.

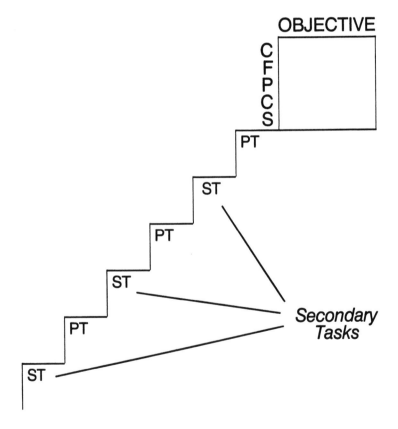

Developing Secondary Tasks

Thus, for Ray, walking/running a mile becomes a secondary or enabling task for running a mile. For example, he may run until he is tired and then walk. He may continue this by progressively running a greater portion of the distance.

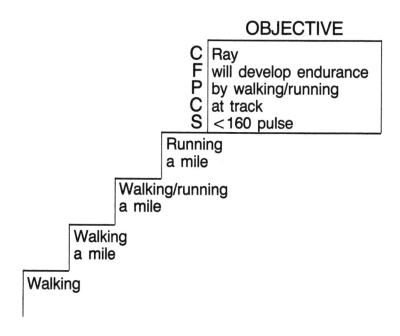

OBJECTIVE

C | Ray
F | will develop endurance
P | by walking/running
C | at track
S | <160 pulse

Running
a mile

Walking/running
a mile

Walking
a mile

Walking

Illustrating Secondary Physical Tasks

Similarly, June requires secondary tasks for her primary personalizing understanding tasks. She needs to be able to respond interchangeably to another person's experience before personalizing the experience. For example, she may begin with one response that functions interchangeably and move progressively to six responses before making personalizing responses.

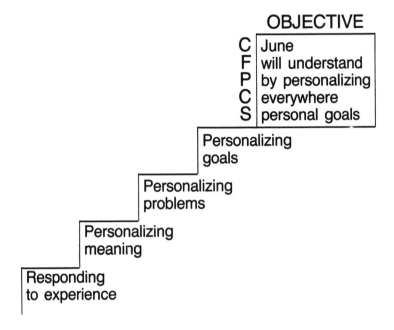

OBJECTIVE

C	June
F	will understand
P	by personalizing
C	everywhere
S	personal goals

Personalizing goals

Personalizing problems

Personalizing meaning

Responding to experience

Illustrating Secondary Emotional Tasks

Further, Ann requires at least one set of secondary or enabling tasks for each primary task. She needs to be able to analyze physical, emotional and intellectual *(PEI)* resource investments before analyzing personal costs. She needs to be able to analyze living, learning and working *(LLW)* benefits before being able to analyze benefits. She needs to be able to analyze the impact of various courses of action upon these costs and benefits before making decisions.

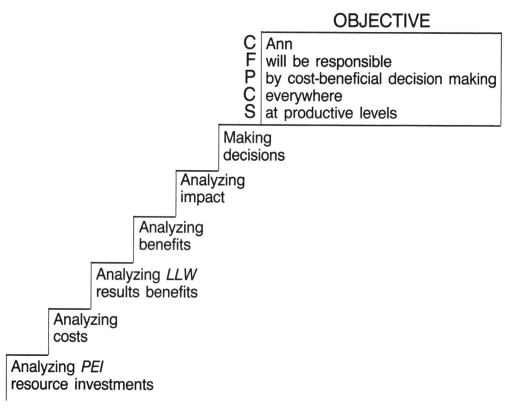

OBJECTIVE

C	Ann
F	will be responsible
P	by cost-beneficial decision making
C	everywhere
S	at productive levels

Making
decisions

Analyzing
impact

Analyzing
benefits

Analyzing *LLW*
results benefits

Analyzing
costs

Analyzing *PEI*
resource investments

Illustrating Secondary Intellectual Tasks

Intermediary Tasks

Intermediary tasks are bridging tasks. They bridge the gaps between the critical primary and/or the enabling secondary tasks. Thus, they may be developed anywhere in the program in order to make the program complete.

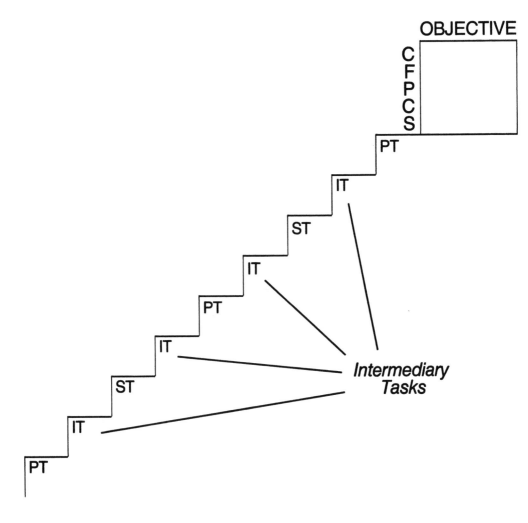

Developing Intermediary Tasks

Thus, for Ray, running a timed mile of increasingly lower times becomes an intermediary or bridging task that completes the program. For example, Ray may begin running a mile in 14 minutes and move progressively downward until he hits ten minutes.

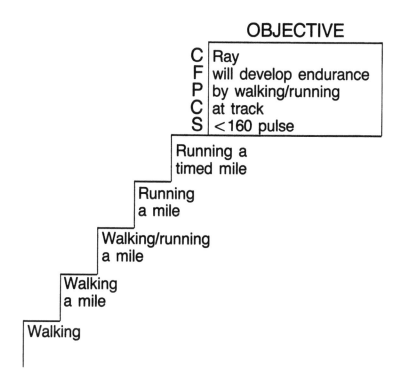

OBJECTIVE

C	Ray
F	will develop endurance
P	by walking/running
C	at track
S	<160 pulse

Running a timed mile

Running a mile

Walking/running a mile

Walking a mile

Walking

Illustrating Intermediary Physical Tasks

Similarly, for June, personalizing changing feelings that come with the movement from problems to goals is an intermediary task in her program. For example, people tend to look forward with excitement and eagerness to achieving their goals, where they once were sad and disappointed about unresolved problems.

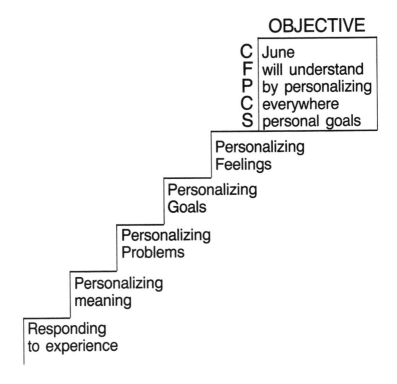

OBJECTIVE

C	June
F	will understand
P	by personalizing
C	everywhere
S	personal goals

Personalizing
Feelings

Personalizing
Goals

Personalizing
Problems

Personalizing
meaning

Responding
to experience

Illustrating Intermediary Emotional Tasks

Further, Ann inserted at least one intermediary task for each secondary task. She wanted to understand the components of values before analyzing resource investments. Also, she wanted to understand the functions of values before analyzing results benefits. Finally, she wanted to expand courses of action before analyzing their impact.

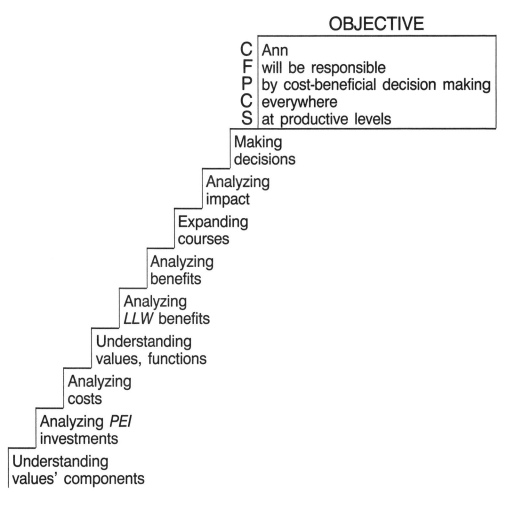

OBJECTIVE

C	Ann
F	will be responsible
P	by cost-beneficial decision making
C	everywhere
S	at productive levels

Making
decisions

Analyzing
impact

Expanding
courses

Analyzing
benefits

Analyzing
LLW benefits

Understanding
values, functions

Analyzing
costs

Analyzing *PEI*
investments

Understanding
values' components

Illustrating Intermediary Intellectual Tasks

You may wish to develop the tasks to achieve one or another of the objectives you have already defined. Simply define the primary, secondary and intermediary tasks needed to achieve your objective. Again, seek out sources of expertise if you are unsure of some of these tasks. You should be able to define every task operationally just as you did your objective.

OBJECTIVE

C
F
P
C
S

In summary, we develop the tasks which we need to perform in order to achieve our objective. These tasks include the primary or critical tasks, secondary or enabling tasks, and intermediary or bridging tasks. We should be able to define each of these tasks operationally. Any objective that can be defined can be achieved by performing tasks that can be defined.

Productive Task Development

5

DEVELOPING STEPS

Stop for a moment! Don't move! Look around you and pick a simple target in the room. Perhaps if you are in a classroom, it is the blackboard or whiteboard. Maybe you could pick a door you would like to exit. Or if you are reading at home, maybe you may pick a nice, comfortable bed upon which you can stretch out and go to sleep. Take a few moments out to develop the steps of a program to get to your target. In other words, develop the steps you will have to take to get to your target.

It can be difficult to succeed in accomplishing this simple mission. Here is a typical program for reaching the target. Most often, people fail on the first step. Among other things, it is too big! Characteristically, they fail to uncross their legs or remove their hand from under their chin. Thus, in most programs, we are defeated before we begin.

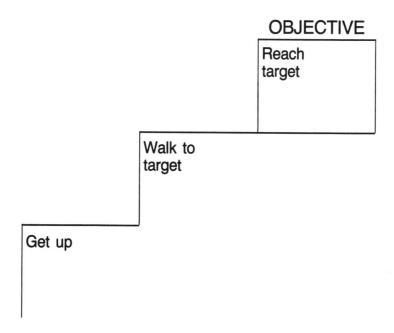

Typical Program

Think about it! All steps to achieving a target objective must be detailed. Here is a productive program for moving from where I am sitting to reach the exit door.

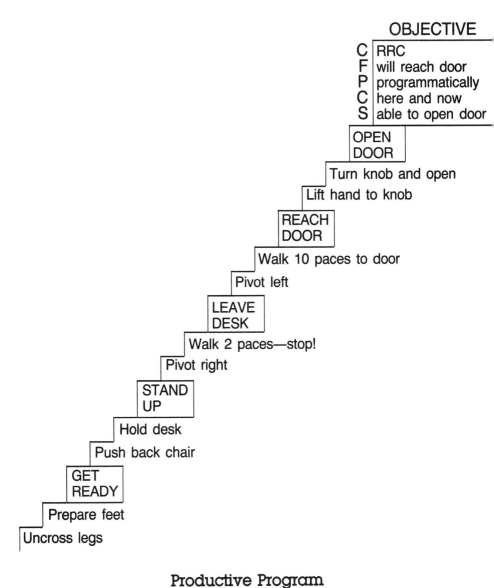

OBJECTIVE

C	RRC
F	will reach door
P	programmatically
C	here and now
S	able to open door

OPEN DOOR

Turn knob and open

Lift hand to knob

REACH DOOR

Walk 10 paces to door

Pivot left

LEAVE DESK

Walk 2 paces—stop!

Pivot right

STAND UP

Hold desk

Push back chair

GET READY

Prepare feet

Uncross legs

Productive Program

Even this program can be broken down in greater detail. We already know that all tasks may be operationally defined in the same manner as the objective. Further, the steps may be too large. For example, the first step of uncrossing legs may be broken down into sub-steps as follows: 1) sit solidly on chair; 2) lift left leg from right; 3) place both feet directly on floor.

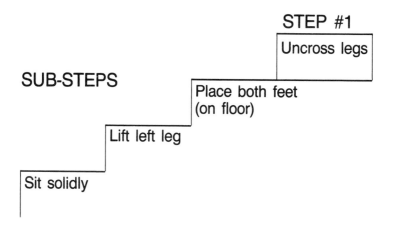

STEP #1

Uncross legs

SUB-STEPS

Place both feet (on floor)

Lift left leg

Sit solidly

The larger point is this: if we have significant difficulty moving programmatically from one position in a room to another, then how much difficulty will we have in achieving important goals in our lives? In order to achieve any objectives, we must develop the tasks to be performed and detail the steps of that performance.

Steps

We develop steps in the same manner that we have developed tasks. First, we define the tasks operationally, just as we did the objective. Next, we develop the steps needed to perform the tasks. Just as with the tasks, the steps also include primary, secondary and intermediary steps.

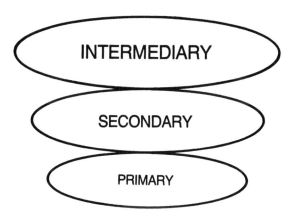

Primary Steps

Again, the primary steps are the critical steps needed to perform the task. For example, in developing his endurance program, Ray's first task was walking. Primary steps in performing the walking task might include actually taking the first step, walking around the house and property, through to walking around the block. Ray would repeat the process of developing primary steps for all of his tasks.

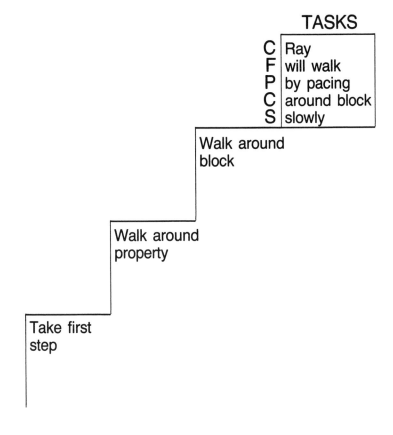

TASKS

C | Ray
F | will walk
P | by pacing
C | around block
S | slowly

Walk around block

Walk around property

Take first step

Illustrating Primary Physical Steps

Similarly, June may define her initial responding task operationally. She may then define her primary steps as responding to content, feeling and meaning. June repeats the process of developing primary steps for all of her tasks.

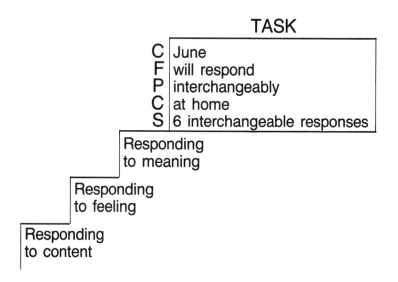

TASK

C	June
F	will respond
P	interchangeably
C	at home
S	6 interchangeable responses

Responding
to meaning

Responding
to feeling

Responding
to content

Illustrating Primary Emotional Steps

Further, Ann's first task may be defined operationally and the steps developed programmatically as follows: acquiring knowledge regarding *PEI* components, *LLW* functions and productivity ratios involved in investing components and achieving functions. Ann repeats the process of developing primary steps for all of her tasks.

TASK

C	Ann
F	will understand values
P	by acquiring knowledge
C	at school
S	at repeatable levels

Acquiring knowledge
of productivity ratios

Acquiring knowledge
of *LLW* functions

Acquiring knowledge
of *PEI* components

Illustrating Primary Intellectual Steps

Secondary Steps

Again, the secondary steps are the enabling steps for the primary steps. For example, Ray may develop a secondary step of preparing to take his first step. This may mean preparing himself physically, emotionally and intellectually. We will elaborate upon this in the section on check steps. Ray repeats the process of developing secondary steps for all of his tasks.

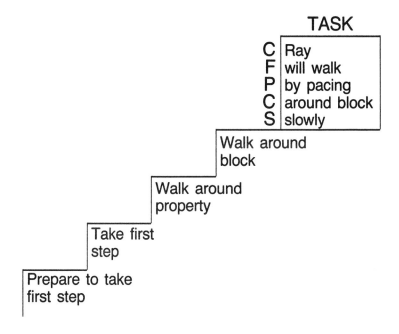

TASK

C	Ray
F	will walk
P	by pacing
C	around block
S	slowly

Walk around block

Walk around property

Take first step

Prepare to take first step

Illustrating Secondary Physical Steps

Similarly, June may develop a secondary enabling step for responding: attending or paying attention to the other person. This may mean attending physically to the other person. June repeats the process of developing secondary steps for all of her tasks.

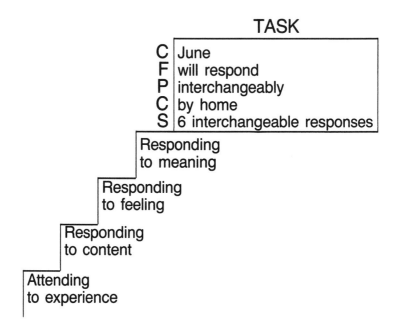

TASK

C	June
F	will respond
P	interchangeably
C	by home
S	6 interchangeable responses

Responding
to meaning

Responding
to feeling

Responding
to content

Attending
to experience

Illustrating Secondary Emotional Steps

Further, Ann may develop a secondary step of acquiring knowledge concerning the definition of values as the meanings we attach to people and things. Ann repeats the process of developing secondary steps for all of her tasks.

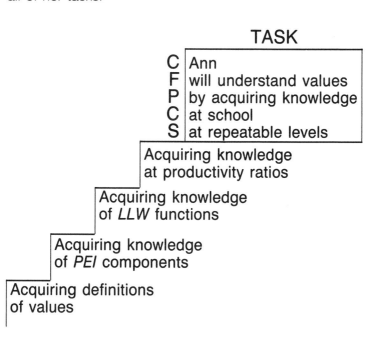

TASK

C	Ann
F	will understand values
P	by acquiring knowledge
C	at school
S	at repeatable levels

Acquiring knowledge
at productivity ratios

Acquiring knowledge
of *LLW* functions

Acquiring knowledge
of *PEI* components

Acquiring definitions
of values

Illustrating Secondary Intellectual Steps

Intermediary Steps

Again, the intermediary steps are the bridging steps for the primary and/or secondary steps. For example, Ray may develop an intermediary step to link the preparatory step and the first step. Ray may require learning the "heel-and-toe" method in order to walk properly.

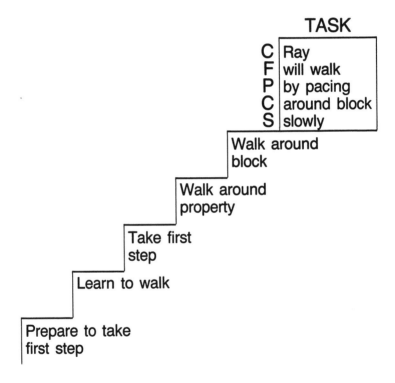

TASK

C	Ray
F	will walk
P	by pacing
C	around block
S	slowly

Walk around block

Walk around property

Take first step

Learn to walk

Prepare to take first step

Illustrating Intermediary Physical Steps

Similarly, June may develop intermediary bridging steps between attending and responding. In order to respond to a person's experience, she must observe the other person and listen to the other person's expressions. June repeats the process of developing intermediary steps for all of her tasks.

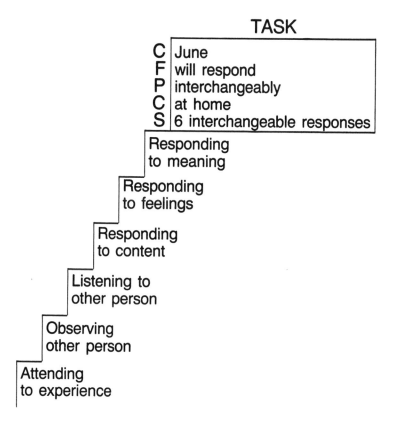

TASK

C	June
F	will respond
P	interchangeably
C	at home
S	6 interchangeable responses

Responding to meaning

Responding to feelings

Responding to content

Listening to other person

Observing other person

Attending to experience

Illustrating Intermediary Emotional Steps

Finally, Ann may develop intermediary steps between her secondary step of defining values and her primary step of acquiring knowledge of physical, emotional and intellectual (*PEI*) components. She may need to learn how to process—explore, understand and act upon—this critical input. Ann repeats the process of developing intermediary steps for all of her tasks.

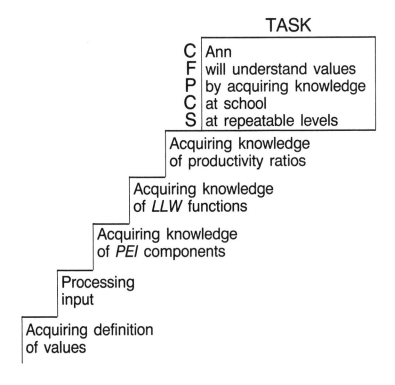

TASK

C Ann
F will understand values
P by acquiring knowledge
C at school
S at repeatable levels

Acquiring knowledge
of productivity ratios

Acquiring knowledge
of *LLW* functions

Acquiring knowledge
of *PEI* components

Processing
input

Acquiring definition
of values

Illustrating Intermediary Intellectual Steps

Again, you may wish to develop the steps to each of your tasks. Define the tasks operationally and develop the primary, secondary and intermediary steps needed to perform the tasks. Seek out sources of expertise if you are unsure of some of the steps.

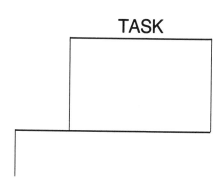

TASK

In summary, we develop the steps which we need to perform our tasks. These steps include primary or critical steps, secondary or enabling steps, and intermediary or bridging steps. We should be able to define every task operationally. Any task that can be defined can be performed implementing programmatic steps. Developing steps prepares us for developing check steps.

Productive Step Development

6

EMPLOYING
CHECK STEPS

How do we know if we are performing our program correctly along the way? Clearly, the standards of the objective alone will not suffice. However, the standards of the tasks will provide a rich source for guiding us. From these standards, we may derive guidelines for check steps or "checking ourselves out." Moreover, how do we know if we are on the right track even before we get started? Again, the definition of the tasks will describe the operations we must prepare for. We can derive the resources we must gather even before we get started.

We may derive *check steps* for "checking ourselves out" from the definition of the standards as follows:

- **Before** check steps for before our implementation of the program.
- **During** check steps for during our implementation of the program;
- **After** check steps for after our implementation of the program.

Together, the *before*, *during* and *after* check steps guide the correct implementation of the program.

Before, During and After Check Steps

Developing Check Steps

Check steps, then, provide us with a means of "checking ourselves out." We may check ourselves out *before, during* or *after* the performance of a task. The *before* check steps emphasize the resources necessary for the performance of the tasks. The *during* check steps emphasize the correctness of the performance. The *after* check steps emphasize the accuracy and completeness of the performance.

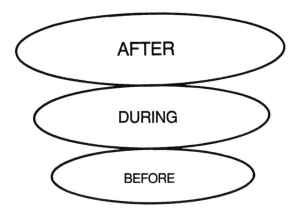

Before Check Steps

The *before* check steps are derived from the definitions of the tasks. They emphasize the physical **(P)**, emotional **(E)** and intellectual **(I)** resources needed to perform the tasks.

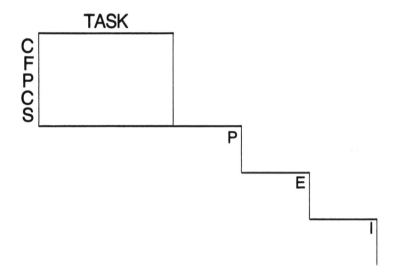

$\mathbf{F}$or example, in order to perform his first walking task, Ray may require the following resources:

Physical
- Running clothes
- Track shoes
- Stop watch and distance markers

Emotional
- Personal motivation and/or incentives
- Personal support person or group

Intellectual
- Definition of task
- Skills and knowledge:
  —Warming up
  —"Heel and toe" walking
  —"Heel and toe" jogging

Similarly, before June initiates her first attending task, she may require the following resources:

Physical
- Another person (surrogate)
- Relevant setting
- Verbal interaction

Emotional
- Personal commitment and/or incentives
- Personal tutor or trainer
- Personal support person or group

Intellectual
- Definition of task
- Skills and knowledge required
  - —Squaring
  - —Leaning
  - —Making eye contact

Illustrating Emotional *Before* Checks

Likewise, Ann may require the following resources before initiating her first values-defining task:

Physical
- Resource materials
- Resource persons
- Specialty resources

Emotional
- Personal commitment and/or incentives
- Personal tutor or trainer
- Personal support person or group

Intellectual
- Definition of task
- Skills and knowledge required
  —Definition of values
  —Values investments
  —Values benefits
  —Values productivity

During Check Steps

The *during* check steps are derived from the standards of the task. They emphasize the correctness of the application of the skills **(S)**, knowledge **(K)**, and attitudes **(A)** in the performance of the task.

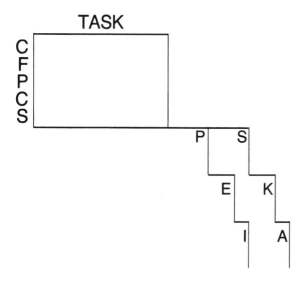

For example, during Ray's performance of his walking and/or running tasks, he may check the correctness of his performance as follows:

- Moving erectly
- Touching "Heel and toe"
- Pumping arms in rhythm
- Feet and arms in opposite rhythm
- Breathing easily and regularly

Illustrating Physical *During* Checks

Similarly, June may check herself out during her performance of initial attending tasks as follows:

- Right shoulder to other person's left shoulder and vice versa
- Leaning at 20° toward the other person while sitting
- Leaning at 10° with one foot slightly forward while standing
- Making eye contact with other person

Illustrating Emotional *Before* Checks

Ann developed the following *during* check steps to guide the correctness of her acquisition of knowledge and skills in cost-beneficial decision-making:

- Defined problems and goals
- Expanded courses of action
- Defined values
- Impact assessments
- Course totals

After Check Steps

The *after* check steps are also derived from the standards of the task. They emphasize the accuracy and completeness of the program **(Pg)** implemented, the performance **(Pe)** given, and the products **(Pd)** produced or the services delivered.

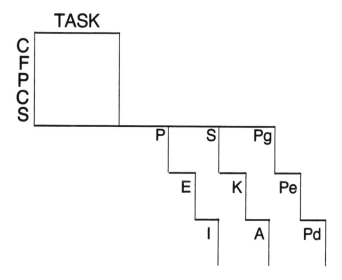

For example, Ray may check out the accuracy and the completeness of his performance of walking and/or running tasks as follows:

- Accurately implemented and completed program steps
- Accurate and complete walking and/or running performance
- Accurate and complete time and distance
- Accurate and complete pulse rate measurement

Illustrating Physical After Checks

Similarly, June may check herself out after demonstrating her attending, responding or personalizing skills:

- Accurately implemented and completed program steps
- Accurate and complete relating performance
- Accurate and complete feedback from the other person

Illustrating Emotional *After* Checks

Finally, Ann may check herself out after she has performed her various cost-beneficial decision-making tasks:

- Minimal resource investment
- Maximum results benefits
- Maximum improvement

You may wish to develop the check steps for your task performance. Simply develop the things you need to do *before, during* and *after* your performance in order to insure your success.

BEFORE:

DURING:

AFTER:

Exercising Check Steps

In summary, the check steps insure the success of our performance. The *before* check steps emphasize the resources we need. The *during* check steps emphasize the correctness of our performance. The *after* check steps emphasize the accuracy and completeness of our performance. Given the guidelines for resources, correctness and completeness, any task can be performed. Employing check steps prepares us for attaching criteria.

7

ATTACHING
CRITERIA

How do we know we have completed our program? Or, put another way, how do we know *when* we have completed our program? There is an obvious answer: when we have achieved our objective. To which we might rejoin: how do we know when we have achieved our objective? The critical answer is: when we have achieved the criteria defined by the objective. The criteria for achievement are defined by the standards of the objective. If all other dimensions are fulfilled, then the criteria of the standards must be achieved.

Attaching Criteria

There is another, implied answer to the question of program conclusion. It is this: we have concluded our program when we have achieved our objective *in the appropriate time.* Time organizes human experience and, thus, human programs. If we present the best application but it is after the deadline, we are likely to fail to achieve our objectives. If we enter a market first, but before it becomes commercial, we may fail to achieve our objectives. Timing can be crucial in life and also in programming *for* life.

Defining Time and Success

Time is the critical dimension of the human condition. Only humans are aware of time. Only humans are guided by time in their life's activities. Indeed, only humans are aware of a beginning and end dictated by time. It makes imminently good sense, then, that human programs are defined by time. Just as we use time to define the distance we have moved in our lives—from our birth, child-rearing, schooling, working, parenting, maturing, through to our death—so do we now use time to help define the milestones of our programs.

Attaching Milestones and Timelines

Designating Milestones

Milestones are the significant tasks we must perform on the way to achieving the objective. They are based upon the tasks developed to achieve the objective. However, they may or may not be the same as these tasks. New tasks that complete the program may be generated.

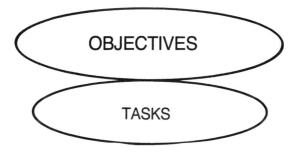

For example, in Ray's physical endurance program, the tasks may be extended from running a timed mile, in any time, to running a mile in successive approximations of ten minutes.

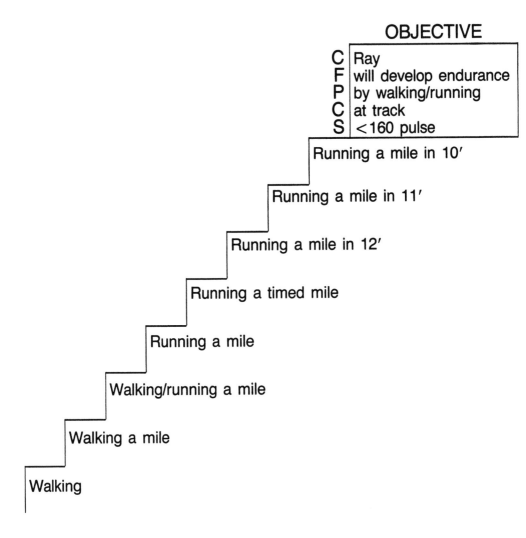

OBJECTIVE

C	Ray
F	will develop endurance
P	by walking/running
C	at track
S	<160 pulse

Running a mile in 10′

Running a mile in 11′

Running a mile in 12′

Running a timed mile

Running a mile

Walking/running a mile

Walking a mile

Walking

Illustrating Physical Milestones

On the other hand, in developing milestones, June collapsed her acquisiton while she expanded her exercising and applying of personalized responses.

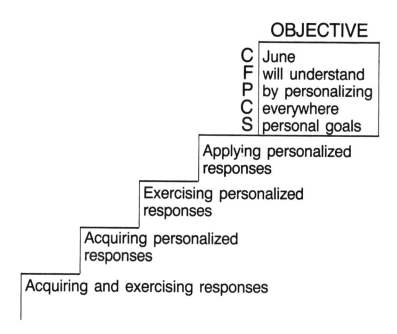

Similarly, Ann collapsed all acquisition of making cost-beneficial decisions while she expanded to exercising, applying and transferring of her acquired responses.

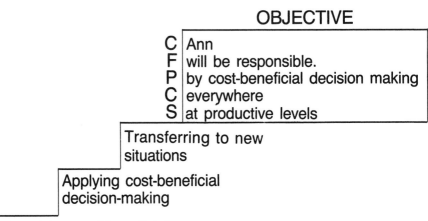

OBJECTIVE

C	Ann
F	will be responsible.
P	by cost-beneficial decision making
C	everywhere
S	at productive levels

Transferring to new
situations

Applying cost-beneficial
decision-making

Exercising cost-beneficial
decision-making

Acquiring cost-beneficial
decision-making

Illustrating Intellectual Milestones

Attaching Timelines

Timelines are simply the times we attach to the milestones. They represent the points at which we anticipate achieving the milestones. We may calculate the times inductively or deductively. We calculate inductively when we build each time contingently upon the previous time. The total time is the time it takes to get to the objective. We calculate deductively when we begin with the total time required to achieve the objective, and then work backward, allocating time to the performance of each required task.

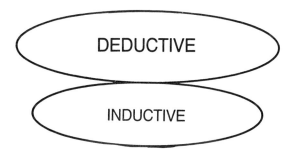

DEDUCTIVE

INDUCTIVE

For example, Ray worked inductively to calculate his physical endurance program. He calculated the amount of time it took to perform each task and sum-totaled the time for the achievement of his objective.

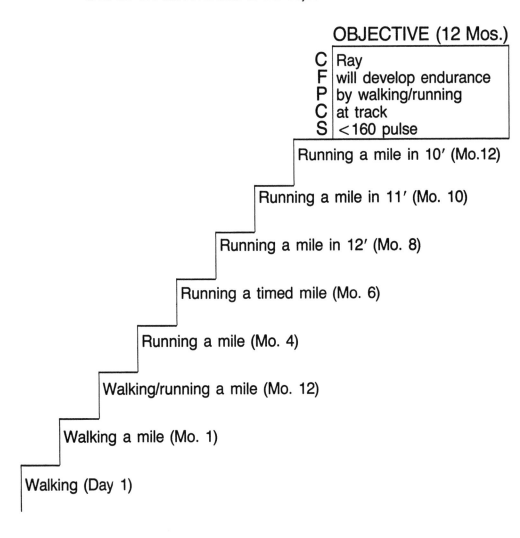

OBJECTIVE (12 Mos.)

C	Ray
F	will develop endurance
P	by walking/running
C	at track
S	<160 pulse

Running a mile in 10' (Mo.12)

Running a mile in 11' (Mo. 10)

Running a mile in 12' (Mo. 8)

Running a timed mile (Mo. 6)

Running a mile (Mo. 4)

Walking/running a mile (Mo. 12)

Walking a mile (Mo. 1)

Walking (Day 1)

Illustrating Physical Timelines

On the other hand, June worked deductively to learn personalizing skills within the month she allowed herself. Then she worked backward to allocate time to the program tasks.

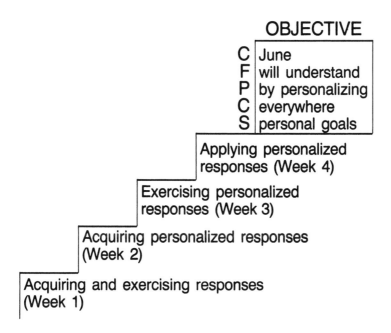

OBJECTIVE

C	June
F	will understand
P	by personalizing
C	everywhere
S	personal goals

Applying personalized responses (Week 4)

Exercising personalized responses (Week 3)

Acquiring personalized responses (Week 2)

Acquiring and exercising responses (Week 1)

Ann also worked deductively, setting a two-month time limit for the achievement of cost-beneficial decision-making skills. Then she allocated time to the different programmatic tasks.

OBJECTIVE

C	Ann
F	will be responsible
P	by cost-beneficial decision making
C	everywhere
S	at productive levels

Transferring to new situations
(Week 8)

Applying cost-beneficial decision making
(Week 3)

Exercising cost-beneficial decision making
(Week 2)

Acquiring cost-beneficial decision making
(Week 1)

Illustrating Intellectual Timelines

Concluding With Objectives

The task milestones, then, become criteria for program performance. The tasks are further defined by the time-lines attached. The ultimate criteria, of course, are the standards for the performance of the objective. The programs conclude with the achievement of the objectives, at the defined levels of standards, within the assigned timelines and limits.

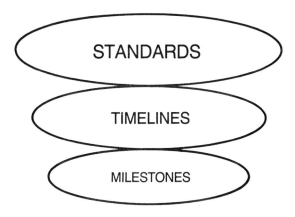

For example, Ray modifies the processes of his objective to incorporate running and walking milestones. In addition, he modifies the standards of his objective to incorporate his twelve-month timeline. He achieves his physical objective when he has achieved all milestones and standards, including timelines.

OBJECTIVE

Components — Ray

Functions — will develop his endurance

Processes — by achieving running and walking milestones so that he will improve his cardio-respiratory coordination

Conditions — at the community track after working hours

Standards — at levels reducing his pulse rate to under 160 for two minutes after exercise and within the twelve-month timeline

Achieving Physical Objectives

Similarly, June modifies her processes to incorporate responding and personalizing milestones, and her standards to incorporate her four-week timeline. She achieves her emotional objective when she has achieved all milestones and all standards, including timelines.

OBJECTIVE

Components	— June in relation to others
Functions	— will learn to understand others
Processes	— by achieving responding and personalizing milestones so that she can relate more productively
Conditions	— at home, school and work
Standards	— at levels that personalize the goals of others and within the four-week timeline

Achieving Emotional Objectives

Finally, Ann also incorporates her milestones and time-lines into the definition of her objective, which she reaches with these achievements.

OBJECTIVE

Components — Ann in relation to others

Functions — will assume responsibilities

Processes — by achieving cost-beneficial decision-making milestones so that she can be productive

Conditions — at home, school and during work

Standards — at the level where she can discharge all of her responsibilities at highly productive levels and within the two-month timeline

You may wish to attach criteria to your programs. You may do so by establishing critical tasks as milestones and attaching timelines. You may also modify your definition of your objective to incorporate the achievement of these milestones and timelines.

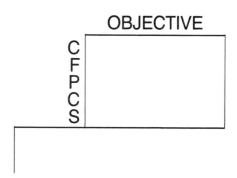

OBJECTIVE

C
F
P
C
S

Exercising Criteria

In summary, we attach criteria in order to direct the development and implementation of our programs. Critical tasks are established as milestones. Timelines are generated inductively and/or deductively. The definition of the objective is modified to incorporate the milestones and timelines. We now have a clear image of where we are going and how long it will take to get there. Attaching criteria prepares us for implementing the program.

Productive Criteria

8

IMPLEMENTING PROGRAMS

What was the last program you developed and implemented? For the moment, do not consider how randomly or non-systematically you may have developed the program. Simply look at the difference between your concept and your implementation. For most programs, the deviation of implementation from intention is enormous. Perhaps it was a good set of intentions that went awry with your spouse, friend, boss or subordinate. Maybe it was a game plan at home, school, work or play that backfired. Often, if not designed productively, the program's implementation fails to accomplish the objective. Indeed, sometimes it accomplishes the opposite.

The differences between design and implementation are usually vast. Many steps are mismanaged and mistaken physically. Many performers are frustrated and impatient emotionally. Many tasks and steps are assumed and distorted intellectually. And these differences between design and implementation are compounded with every step. This is why the programs we implement with our loved ones at home, our learners in school and our employees at work often fail to achieve the desired results. Yet there are safeguards or "insurance policies" that we can take against dysfunctional implementation.

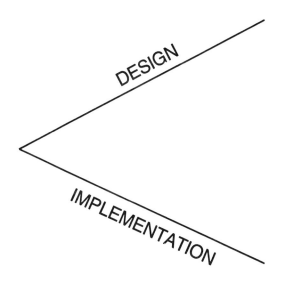

**Differences Between Design
and Implementation**

Mastery Steps

We may call these safeguards *mastery steps* because they insure the implementation of the program. We master the program by moving to the next task dependent upon the successful completion of the last task. This principle of advancement to new tasks *only* after mastering previous tasks is the key to successfully achieving objectives. The mastery steps include reviewing and reciting, rehearsing and revising, realizing and reinforcing and, finally, repeating the tasks until they are mastered.

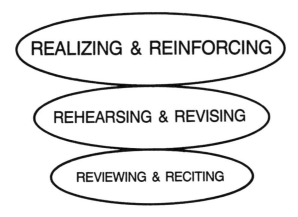

REALIZING & REINFORCING

REHEARSING & REVISING

REVIEWING & RECITING

In this context, we review and recite the program in order to insure our intimate acquaintance with its objectives, tasks, steps, milestones and timelines. We rehearse and revise the program in order to remedy its vulnerabilities and insure its comprehensiveness. Moreover, we realize and reinforce the implementation of the program in order to insure its accuracy and effectiveness. Finally, we repeat the tasks and steps until we have mastered them.

Repeat Mastery Steps

Reviewing and Reciting

Reviewing and reciting are the first safeguards against improper or dysfunctional implementation of the program. Reviewing emphasizes summarizing the contingency tasks and steps. The basic principle of review is this: upon addressing each new task, we review all contingent tasks and steps. Reviewing enables us to identify any weaknesses in previous learnings.

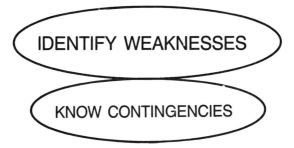

IDENTIFY WEAKNESSES

KNOW CONTINGENCIES

One way of insuring reviewing is reciting. Reciting the contingency tasks and steps out loud insures familiarity with them. Having someone else check out the accuracy of the recitation provides valuable feedback. Reciting enables us to strengthen and reinforce our foundation for task performance.

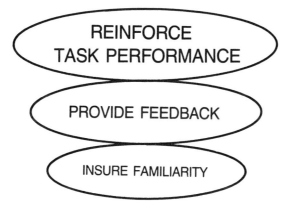

Reciting

Ann, June and Ray mastered the tasks of their program by reviewing and reciting every previous task upon the introduction to each new task. For Ann, this meant reviewing and reciting all previous cost-beneficial decision-making tasks upon the introduction to each new task. For June, this meant reviewing and reciting all responding and personalizing tasks upon the introduction to each new task. Finally, for Ray, this meant reviewing and reciting all walking/running tasks as he moved toward more refined tasks involving milestones and timelines.

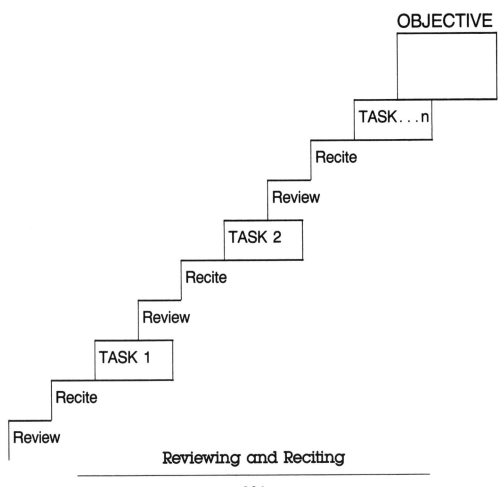

Reviewing and Reciting

Rehearsing and Revising

The basic principle of rehearsing is this: upon the introduction of each new task, we practice the behaviors we wish to realize or enact. Rehearsing the tasks simply means practicing the behaviors in a preliminary way before attempting to realize them in real life. Rehearsing increases the probability of succeeding at any one task.

$\mathbf{A}$gain, rehearsing the program enables us to assess its vulnerabilities and comprehensiveness. Thus, we can revise the program to remedy its weaknesses. We can redefine inappropriately defined tasks. We can fill in missing tasks and steps or extend others. In this manner, we develop a complete and accurate program to achieve our objective.

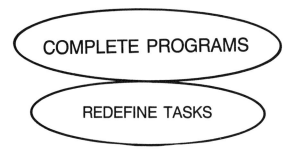

Ann, June and Ray mastered the tasks of their programs by rehearsing and revising them prior to their performance. Ann and June found that rehearsal and revision were particularly critical in the later stages of their programs. Ray found that, in effect, each step of his running program was the rehearsal for the next.

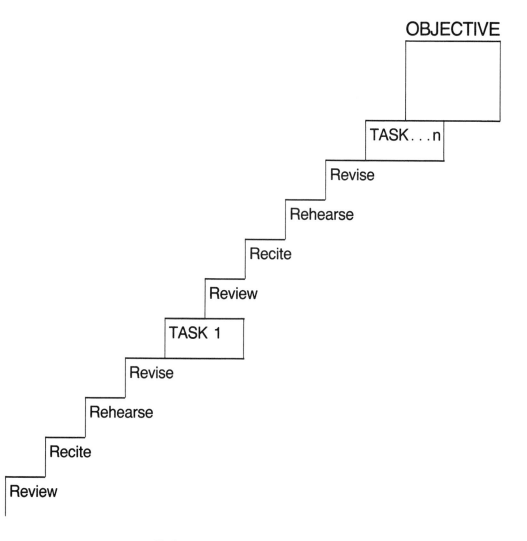

Rehearsing and Revising

Realizing and Reinforcing

The principle of realizing or enacting the program is this: upon addressing each new task, we follow the precise steps of its performance. That way, we increase the probability of succeeding in achieving our objective. At a minimum, we test the effectiveness of our program in achieving our objective.

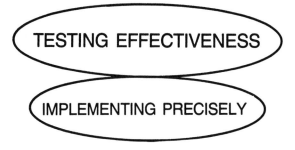

We can further insure realizing our program precisely by reinforcing our performance. Positive or goal-directed performance is rewarded. Poor or aimless performance or non-performance is ignored or punished. Performance that is not clear immediately is observed carefully.

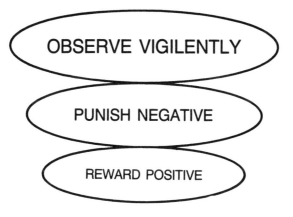

$\mathbf{A}$nn, June and Ray mastered their programs by rewarding themselves for the successful realization of their tasks. Operating from their own unique frames of reference, June allowed herself to buy articles of grooming and dress, Ray awarded himself recreational money, and Ann simply took a moment to reflect on her pride in accomplishment.

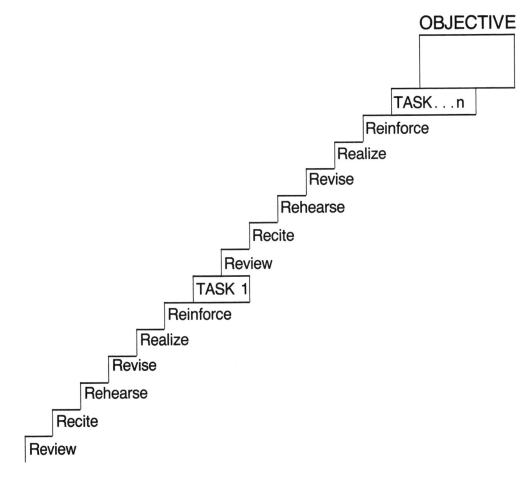

Realizing and Reinforcing

Finally, after all other implementation steps are taken, we use the principle of repetition: upon performance of the task, we continue to perform the task until we have achieved our intended standards. Repetition until excellence is reached is the cornerstone of mastery, whether in a cardio-vascular endurance program, a personalizing understanding program, or a cost-beneficial decision-making program.

Repeating

You may, if you wish, exercise your program implementation skills. Simply employ the "Seven R's (reviewing, reciting, rehearsing, revising, realizing, reinforcing and repeating) of Implementing" to your program tasks.

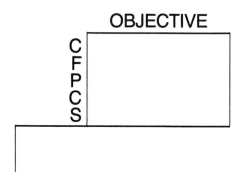

OBJECTIVE

C
F
P
C
S

Exercising Program Implementation

In summary, we review and recite to insure knowledge of contingencies and weaknesses. We rehearse and revise in order to practice behaviors and insure comprehensiveness. We realize and reinforce in order to implement precisely and test effectiveness. Finally, we repeat until we reach mastery. Any program that can be developed systematically can be implemented precisely.

9

PPD
IMPLICATIONS

We have not fully discharged our responsibilities to ourselves until we have developed and implemented our program. We have not fully discharged our responsibilities to others until we have developed and implemented programs with them. Program development is the first step to responsibility. As soon as we set an objective, we have made a judgment to accomplish something. We can be held accountable, *humanly* accountable! The choice to succeed or fail is now conscious. The answer is reflected in the quality of the program we develop to achieve our objective. It is not possible to change behavior or expand human experience without a program.

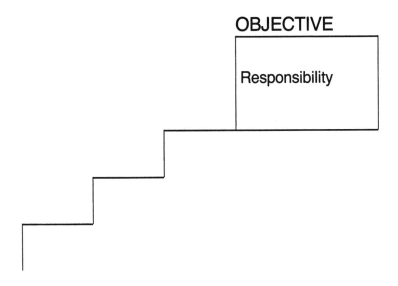

OBJECTIVE

Responsibility

Productive Program Development

There are many different ways of viewing program development, and the implications of each are profound. The most basic involves developing all of the tasks necessary to achieve an objective. The principle involves turning each task into an objective and then developing the steps to the new objective. In turn, each of the steps can be treated like an objective, at which point still smaller steps can be developed to achieve that. For example, interpersonal attending may be broken down into attending physically, observing and listening. And attending physically, in turn, may be broken down into squaring, leaning and eye contact. The same is true for an attentive reading posture program. Remember?! This process can continue until all of the steps needed to achieve the objective have been detailed. Indeed, the process may be continued until we have developed one continuous series of steps to our goals. The point at which we stop developing steps has to do with success probabilities and how much we are betting on achieving our goal. The more steps we develop, the higher the probability of succeeding. The more we are betting on succeeding, the more steps we must develop to increase the probability of succeeding. If we are betting our lives, we will not want to leave out a step. Every day, we bet the lives of our children, our students, our clients, our employees. Let us not leave out a step.

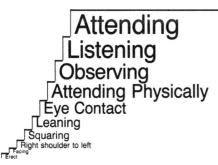

Attending
Listening
Observing
Attending Physically
Eye Contact
Leaning
Squaring
Right shoulder to left
Facing
Erect

Every Step Becomes a Goal in a Smaller Program

From another view, every objective may become a step in a larger program. Every program, whether explicitly or implicitly, is related to larger programs. For example, attending skills objectives become interpersonal skills tasks; interpersonal skills objectives become living skills tasks; living skills objectives become learning skills tasks; learning skills objectives become working skills tasks. In a very real sense, program development defines directionality. If we do not have the full picture in mind when we begin, it will unfold for us as we complete the steps in it. If we say "A," we must say "B" and "C" and "D" and so on. A program is the first step of an efficient, although lengthy, journey to fulfillment.

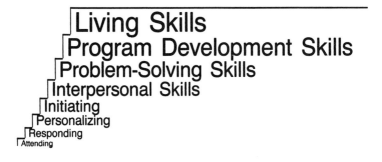

Living Skills
Program Development Skills
Problem-Solving Skills
Interpersonal Skills
Initiating
Personalizing
Responding
Attending

Every Goal Becomes a Step in a Larger Program

In turn, every program becomes a mere step in a larger system. For example, programs in living, learning and working skills are merely steps in programs of management, community development, and national and international development. Program development is the only vehicle for increasing responsibility and direction. It alone allows us to throw out our "sky hooks" and rise above our supposed human limitations. There is no freedom without programs, only political expedience! Without programs, we are prisoners of our history. And that history bodes darkly.

International Development
National Development
Community Development Skills
Management Skills
Working Skills
Learning Skills
Living Skills

Every Program Becomes a Step in a Larger System

Developmental Consequences

Most important, we can grow with a program. Indeed, only a program which expands our experience and skills can free us of the limits of our own potential. Only a program provides us with the feedback necessary to improve our functioning. All it takes to grow is a program for growth. All it takes to develop a growth program is an achievable human goal and a lot of hard work. The work involved in developing a program is the price paid for knowing what works and what doesn't— what is relevant and what is not. Those who pay that price will be proud of their humanity and accountable for it. They comprehend fully the freedom that comes only with complete, efficient actions based upon what they understand. By acting, they learn more about what they know and do not know. Those who will not pay the price talk only about "never really knowing anything for sure." And they are correct!

Where you want to be

Where you are

Growing

Programs alone take us to where we want to be. Good programs take us from where we think we are to where we want to be. Having goals without good programs to achieve these goals is the same as having no direction at all. In this regard, many things which we call programs are not programs at all. Either their goals are not achievable or steps are missing. Or most important, no one can be held accountable. Responsibility for outcome is a critical index of a good program. If we have programs for getting us to where we want to be, what we know is less likely to be misused, abused, ignored or neutralized by ourselves or others. If we do not have programs, we cannot even judge the programs of others, because we cannot judge what we have not mastered. If we do not have the responses to act, we do not really have the discriminating ability to judge. We can only look for the vulnerabilities in others. We can only move to corrupt others people's hard work.

Where We Want to Be

It is intrinsic in the nature of programs that they keep us moving over our lifetimes, and further! A good program, because it is transmittable, survives us. Where we want to be becomes where we are when we get there. This is the key principle of program development that keeps us moving. There are no plateaus. Only a lifetime of hard work and full living! When we have acted to get from where we are to where we want to be, then where we wanted to be becomes where we are. In order to continue growing we must recycle exploration, understanding and action. We start all over again!

GOAL #2

Where you want to be

GOAL #1

Where you are

Where You Want to Be Becomes
Where You Are When You Get There

Just as the programs *begin* with where we are, so do they *end* with where we are. They come around full circle. But, they leave us functioning at a higher level than when we began. And they leave us in greater contact with where we are. Where we *think* we are converges with where we are. And we have a more realistic "jumping off" spot for going from where we are to still higher levels, where we want or need to be. But we must follow a program to get there, and not an imitation or distortion of someone else's program.

We must achieve before we can create. We must be helped before we can help. If we do not have programs for ourselves, we are not really fit to help others. We can only contribute when we are, indeed, functioning at the contributor level. We are only free of the program when we have conquered it.

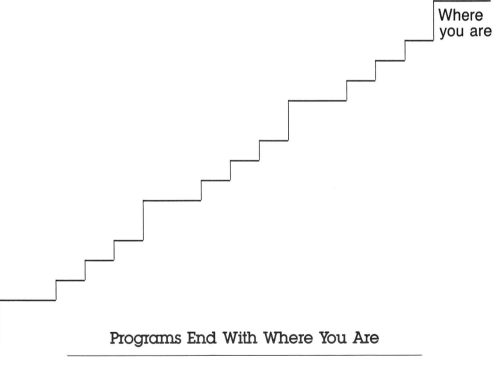

Where you are

Programs End With Where You Are

And then we begin again, for ourselves and for others! We are free of our programs to the extent that we can train others to get to where we are. We are free of what we know when we can teach someone else all we know. Only then can we learn something new. Only then can we create new functions, and new technology. Programs are the product of technology. People are the product of programs. And technology is the product of people. There are no lasting solutions other than technological solutions. There is no lasting effectiveness other than programmatic effectiveness.

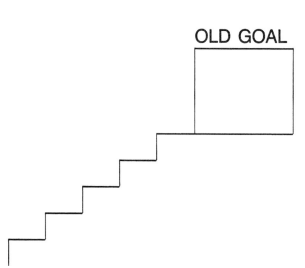

NEW GOAL

OLD GOAL

...And Then Begin Again

In one hand, we bring our life process skills, including program development skills. In the other hand, we must bring expertise in a specialty area. In order to develop effective programs, we must acquire expertise in a specialty area. In order to acquire expertise in a specialty area, we must develop effective programs. One cannot grow without the other. That is why we've structured this book with physical, emotional and intellectual skills development. Because program development—like marriage—may be "for better or worse." It all depends upon who has the power and what she knows.

...And Again

THE ONLY WINNING STRATEGY IS PROGRAMMATIC

APPENDIX

PRODUCTIVE PROGRAM
DEVELOPMENT OVERVIEW

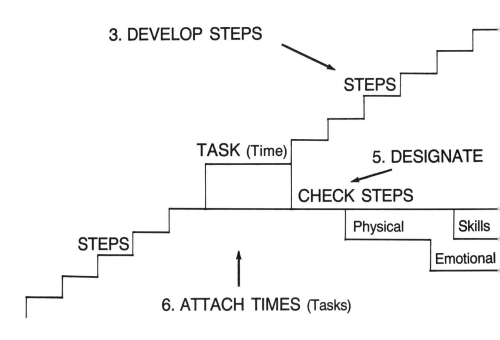

2. DEFINE TASKS

3. DEVELOP STEPS

STEPS

TASK (Time)

5. DESIGNATE

CHECK STEPS

Physical Skills

Emotional

STEPS

6. ATTACH TIMES (Tasks)

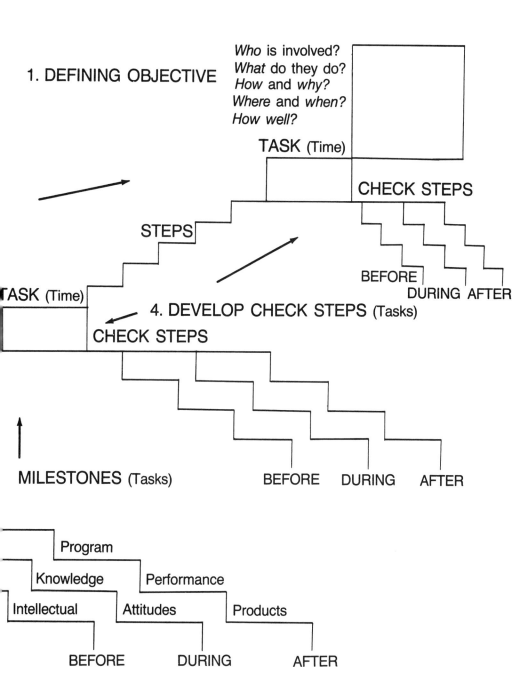

1. DEFINING OBJECTIVE

Who is involved?
What do they do?
How and *why*?
Where and *when*?
How well?

TASK (Time)

CHECK STEPS

STEPS

BEFORE
DURING AFTER

TASK (Time)

4. DEVELOP CHECK STEPS (Tasks)

CHECK STEPS

MILESTONES (Tasks)   BEFORE   DURING   AFTER

Program

Knowledge   Performance

Intellectual   Attitudes   Products

BEFORE   DURING   AFTER

163

NOTES

NOTES

NOTES

NOTES

NOTES